Super Crosswords for Kids

Trip Payne

Official
American Mensa
Puzzle Book

Sterling Publishing Co., Inc.
New York

Dedicated to
Mike Shenk, Will Shortz, and Stan Newman—
the people who gave me a chance in the puzzle world
back when I was still a kid.

Also by Trip Payne

Crosswords for Kids
Great Crosswords for Kids
Crosswords to Strain Your Brain
Mighty Mini Crosswords
365 Mind-Challenging Crosswords
The Little Giant Encyclopedia of Word Puzzles (coauthor)

Edited by Peter Gordon

2 4 6 8 10 9 7 5 3

Published by Sterling Publishing Co., Inc.
387 Park Avenue South, NY 10016
© 2003 by Trip Payne
Distributed in Canada by Sterling Publishing
C/o Canadian Manda Group, One Atlantic Avenue, Suite 105
Toronto, Ontario, Canada M6K 3E7
Distributed in Great Britain and Europe by Chris Lloyd at Orca Book Services
Stanley House, Fleets Lane, Poole BH15 3AJ England
Distributed in Australia by Capricorn Link (Australia) Pty. Ltd.
P.O. Box 704, Windsor, NSW 2756 Australia

Sterling ISBN 0-8069-9290-5

CONTENTS

INTRODUCTION

Do you like mystery stories? If so, you'll probably like crossword puzzles. Like in a mystery, you have to follow the clues to get the answers. Also, you have to use logic—if you can't figure out the clue for one word, maybe you can figure out the clues for the words that cross it.

At the end of solving a puzzle, though, you don't have a big scene where you announce who the criminal is. You have a filled-in grid that proves you were able to solve every clue that came your way!

So when you're ready, turn the page and begin solving your first "case"—Puzzle 1!

—Trip Payne

PUZZLES

1

ACROSS

1 It holds back water in a river
4 Final
8 Hit in the face
12 ___ Baba
13 "___ silly question ...": 2 words
14 Mexican coin
15 ___ Weasley (Harry Potter's best friend)
16 Type of Girl Scout cookies: 2 words
18 One of ___ days (sometime soon)
20 ___ Agassi (famous tennis player)
21 "Every cloud ___ silver lining": 2 words
22 "Do as ___!" ("Obey me!"): 2 words
25 Letters that mean "We need help!"
26 Type of Girl Scout cookies: Hyphenated
29 Start of the alphabet
32 Trucks that people use when they have to move
33 Plays a part on stage
37 Woolly animal from South America
39 She's Lucy's best friend on "I Love Lucy"
40 Type of Girl Scout cookies
44 Tool that's used to chop wood
45 Word at the end of a prayer
46 Cry
47 Sticky stuff that comes out of a tree
48 Baseball team from Cincinnati
49 Not odd
50 It means "most" when it's at the end of a word

DOWN

1 ___ Vader (character in "Star Wars")
2 It means both "hello" and "goodbye" in Hawaii
3 Underground places where people dig for gold
4 Not on time
5 What's left after something is burned
6 Enjoy a certain winter sport
7 Light brown color
8 Twirl around
9 ___ a hand (helps out)

Crossword Grid

1	2	3	■	4	5	6	7	■	8	9	10	11
12			■	13				■	14			
15			■	16			17					
18			19		■	■	20					
21				■	22	23	24		■	25		
■	■		26	27				■	28		■	■
29	30	31	■	32				■	33	34	35	36
37			38		■	■	39					
40				41	42	43		■	44			
45				■	46			■	47			
48				■	49			■	50			

10 George Jetson's pet dog

11 What an artist's model does

17 White sandwich spread, for short

19 Downhearted

22 "This ___ stick-up!": 2 words

23 A preacher might have a sermon about it

24 Commercials

27 ___ Office (where the president works)

28 Rested in a chair

29 Part of a church where people get married

30 Hold responsible for something going wrong

31 Cooped up, like a canary

34 Pursue

35 State where Houston and Dallas are

36 Took a nap

38 "A dog is ___ best friend"

39 Cable channel that's all about sports: Abbreviation

41 Have a debt

42 Its capital is Carson City: Abbreviation

43 "___ whiz!"

2

ACROSS

1 Frying ___
4 Knock softly on a door
7 Speak
10 Gets older
12 "How was ___ know?": 2 words
13 Three times three
14 Extinct bird, or a stupid person
15 Where you put a napkin when you eat
16 Finds the total
17 ___ as a pancake
19 Border
21 Punctuation mark between the 3's in 3:30
23 "Not ___ long shot!": 2 words
24 "Under the ___" (song from "The Little Mermaid")
27 "Humpty Dumpty sat ___ wall": 2 words
28 Bottom color in a stoplight
30 Frosty the Snowman wore one
31 ___ Affleck (famous actor)
32 It's on top of a jar
33 Taking out the garbage, for example

35 Changes the color of hair
37 Cat's sound
38 Thought
40 What the bride and groom say at a wedding: 2 words
42 Do as you're told
45 Piece of silverware
46 Negative answers
47 Bird that represents peace
48 "___ about time!"
49 "___ a load of this!"
50 Wager

DOWN

1 Lily ___
2 A long time ___
3 Homer's neighbor on "The Simpsons": 2 words
4 What a pinball machine says if you shake it too much
5 One ___ time (not in groups): 2 words
6 Spinach-eating sailor man
7 Krusty's assistant on "The Simpsons": 2 words

8 Tom ___ Jerry
9 What a nod means
11 Without anyone else's help
13 Old horse
18 It's measured with a protractor
20 Waltz or fox trot, for example
21 Corn on the ___
22 Last number in a countdown
23 It comes in "single," "full," "queen," and "king" sizes

25 Hearing organ
26 Had a snack
29 Going upward
34 Little Red Riding ___
36 Big, hairy animal from Asia
37 Almost all
38 "___ Ran the Circus" (Dr. Seuss book): 2 words
39 Part of a lowercase letter I
41 Female deer
43 New Year's ___
44 So far

3

ACROSS

1 Cassettes
6 Sense of humor
9 Container that might have a cork in the top
12 "Carmen" is a famous one
13 Go ___ diet: 2 words
14 America, for short
15 ___ badge (what a Scout earns)
16 The Grinch's pet dog
17 ___ talk (speech that a team's coach gives to the players)
18 It gets rid of a disease
20 "Not ___ can help it!": 2 words
22 You might spread it on toast
25 Sprints
27 Keep ___ (don't give up): 2 words
30 The Atlantic and Pacific, for example
32 What a groom usually wears at his wedding
34 Uncool person
35 Rip
37 Straight line
38 You can buy them at a music store: Abbreviation
40 Snatch
42 Paper that says you owe someone money

44 The fifth month of the year
46 The sound a horse makes
50 It's used to pave roads
51 Mind-reading ability, for short
52 Loosen a shoelace
53 Where the sun and moon are
54 Have dinner
55 Rock

DOWN

1 ___ Cruise (famous actor)
2 Gorilla
3 Miles ___ hour (how a car's speed is measured)
4 The name of the prince in "The Little Mermaid"
5 Planet with big rings around it
6 Grown-up girls
7 ___ good mood (happy): 2 words
8 Cab
9 Planet known for its large Red Spot
10 "What's the ___?" ("It doesn't matter")
11 The space where a tooth came out

19 The Tin Woodman's problem in "The Wizard of Oz"

21 One way to send a document

22 Garfield's owner, in the comic strip

23 The highest card in many card games

24 The closest planet to the sun

26 Celebrity

28 "What can ___ to help?": 2 words

29 ___ truck (vehicle that picks up stranded cars)

31 Find a sum

33 The first planet to be discovered with a telescope

36 Country where the Great Pyramids are

39 Captain Hook's sidekick in "Peter Pan"

41 Crooked

42 "___ no wonder!"

43 Tree that acorns come from

45 Thin ___ rail: 2 words

47 "Who am ___ say?": 2 words

48 ___ rummy (card game)

49 ___-haw (donkey's sound)

4

ACROSS

1 "Give ___ break!":
2 words
4 50%
8 Price ___ (things that tell how much items cost)
12 Stimpy's pal, in cartoons
13 India is on this continent
14 Black-and-white cookie
15 Water-___ (have fun on a lake)
16 October 31
18 Nasty
20 Cable channel that shows news all the time: Abbreviation
21 What you put your cafeteria food on
23 One of the Seven Dwarfs
24 "Hansel ___ Gretel"
27 February 14: 2 words
31 What drivers drive on: Abbreviation
32 Female sheep
33 Side of a knife
34 "___ was saying ...":
2 words
35 Someone whose pants are on fire?
37 December 25
41 Finish

44 Male pig
45 Walking stick
46 Polite thing to call a man
47 Uses a needle and thread
48 "Dr. Jekyll and Mr. ___"
49 Secret agent

DOWN

1 "___ Doubtfire" (Robin Williams movie)
2 What someone might say when they see a mouse
3 Zoo residents
4 Sound of laughter: Hyphenated
5 Strong ___ ox: 2 words
6 Girl on "Rugrats"
7 Bird of prey
8 Small city
9 "You ___ My Sunshine" (old song)
10 "___ whillikers!" ("Gosh!")
11 Daughter's brother
17 "___ upon a time ..."
19 Part of the body where the pupil is
21 VCRs are hooked up to them: Abbreviation

22 Animal that's similar to a mouse

23 "If I should ___ before I wake ..."

24 What you write on an envelope

25 Worthless horse

26 You color Easter eggs with it

28 The Loch ___ Monster (beast in Scotland)

29 Move a muscle

30 Body of water

34 ___ out (freshens in the breeze)

35 Never-Never ___ (Peter Pan's home)

36 "Peekaboo, ___ you!": 2 words

37 Television network on which "Everybody Loves Raymond" can be seen: Abbreviation

38 Gardening tool

39 Uncooked

40 Mother ___ I (playground game)

42 Small bite

43 Use a towel

5

ACROSS

1 A baby wears it around its neck
4 You might wear one after a bath
8 What hospital food is served on
12 How old you are
13 Barge ___ (interrupt): 2 words
14 "Cross my heart and ___ to die"
15 Something to drink in winter: 2 words
17 Mothers of lambs
18 The path a mail carrier follows: Abbreviation
19 Guys
21 The Golden ___ ("Do unto others ...")
24 Slippery fish
25 "___ was going to St. Ives ...": 2 words
28 Something to do in winter: 2 words
32 What a broken-down car might need
33 Where the elbow is
34 Some children
35 "And so on": Abbreviation
36 Gobbled up
38 What the Ugly Duckling turned into

41 Something to ride in winter
46 Not soft
47 ___ instant (very quickly): 2 words
48 Ginger ___ (kind of drink)
49 They see
50 Morse ___
51 A little ___ (small amount)

DOWN

1 "___, humbug!" (what Scrooge said)
2 "Where do ___ from here?": 2 words
3 Gamble
4 A large group of people going wild
5 Less than twice
6 What a ghost says
7 The hard part of a tooth
8 Every now and ___ (sometimes)
9 "... and pretty maids all in a ___"
10 Big, hairy animal
11 "I agree"
16 All the people who work on a ship

20 One of Santa's helpers
21 Letters after Q
22 Game with colorful cards
23 Opposite of high
24 Kind of tree
25 Long ___ (in the past)
26 Not outgoing
27 "___ my pleasure"
29 A baseball player swings one
30 One of the four oceans
31 "___ your pardon!": 2 words
35 Concludes

36 In ___ mood (upset): 2 words
37 Dial ___ (sound you hear on the phone)
38 That girl
39 Milky ___ (the Earth's galaxy)
40 "How ___ you?"
42 Yoko ___ (singer who was married to John Lennon)
43 Talk a lot
44 Muhammad ___ (famous boxer)
45 It's in the center of a Ping-Pong table

6

ACROSS

1 "How ___ you say such a thing?"
6 Do some arithmetic
9 You might build a model from one
12 Musical that includes the song "Tomorrow"
13 U.S. group that uses spies: Abbreviation
14 Large bird from Australia
15 The only president to be elected four times
17 Old, useless horse
18 It can follow "lemon" or "orange" in names of drinks
19 What Jack Sprat's wife couldn't eat
21 ___ Blanc (man who did the voice of Bugs Bunny)
24 Taste a drink
26 Command to a dog
29 The opposite of good
31 Boy
33 A sword has a sharp one
34 They determine the color of your eyes, how tall you are, etc.
36 "You bet!"
38 Money used in Japan
39 Layer of paint

41 Had lunch
43 Scooby-___
45 President who wrote the Declaration of Independence
50 Bird that hoots
51 "Th-th-that's ___, folks!"
52 Beethoven's instrument
53 Perfect score in gymnastics
54 It opens a lock
55 Tunnel underneath a city

DOWN

1 Automobile
2 Yoko ___ (Japanese singer)
3 Card game with "Skip" and "Reverse" cards
4 One of the kids on "The Simpsons"
5 Ownership cards in Monopoly
6 Part of a royal flush, in poker
7 ___ pickle
8 Goes out with
9 The youngest person ever elected president
10 "___ little teapot ...": 2 words

11 Pull hard

16 What a bride wears over her face

20 Larger relative of a monkey

21 One of the sisters in "Little Women"

22 Christmas ___

23 President during the U.S. Civil War

25 "___ attention!"

27 It gets bigger on your birthday

28 Barbie's boyfriend

30 Zodiac sign whose symbol is a lion

32 Unable to hear

35 Pat ___ (the host of "Wheel of Fortune")

37 Parts of a staircase

40 What the T in TV stands for

42 One of the five Great Lakes

43 Wakko and Yakko's sister, on "Animaniacs"

44 Need to pay back

46 Ride in an airplane

47 Cutting tool

48 "I'm having ___ of those days"

49 Neither here ___ there

7

ACROSS

1 Fathers
5 Baby ___ (pal of Barney the dinosaur)
8 Remain
12 "Yeah, sure!": 2 words
13 ___ Grande (river in Texas)
14 Large lake near Pennsylvania
15 Game where you try to find a place to sit: 2 words
18 Use scissors
19 First-aid ___ (box that contains bandages)
20 Not sleeping
23 Teacher's ___ (someone the teacher especially likes)
24 Busta Rhymes makes this kind of music
27 What baseball players wear on their heads
28 Welcome ___ (something to wipe your feet on)
29 "In ___ of emergency, break glass"
30 The calm center of a hurricane
31 Kind of grain
32 Lady
33 "A Nightmare on ___ Street" (famous horror movie)
34 "Do you know who ___?": 2 words
35 Game where you try to identify people without seeing them: 2 words
42 ___ the rules (come close to cheating)
43 Paintings and sculptures
44 The largest continent
45 Sail the seven ___
46 One of the signs of the zodiac
47 What a camper sleeps in

DOWN

1 Opposite of bright
2 The monkey in the movie "Aladdin"
3 ___ Moines (the capital of Iowa)
4 "___ and stones may break my bones ..."
5 Spoiled kid
6 ___ and vinegar (salad topping)
7 Where you might hold your wallet
8 ___ belt (strap in a car)
9 Prefix for "cycle" or "angle"
10 It's inside a basketball

11 Not "no" or "maybe"
16 A pool player uses one
17 Strike
20 Good card to have in blackjack
21 "No ___, José!"
22 Big jungle animal
23 ___ on the back (kind of encouragement)
24 Male sheep
25 Clear ___ bell: 2 words
26 It's filled with ink
28 The kind of animal a dog or an elephant is
29 War
31 "This ___ man, he played one ..."

32 "Fuzzy Wuzzy ___ a bear"
33 Stops
34 Vanish ___ thin air
35 Pellets in toy guns
36 Robert E. ___ (general in the Civil War)
37 "... partridge ___ pear tree": 2 words
38 "What ___ you talking about?"
39 "What's the ___ in trying?" (quitter's question)
40 Part of a shark
41 Overweight

8

ACROSS

1 It usually grows on the north side of trees
5 Tick-___ (clock sound)
9 "That's amazing!"
12 Creature in "Return of the Jedi"
13 Sound effect you could hear in a canyon
14 Female animal that gives wool
15 Large, dangerous reptile
17 Snack for an aardvark
18 ___ for the course (typical)
19 They might need to be housebroken
21 "The Cat in the ___"
24 Last ___ not least
26 ___ of schedule (early)
29 Spin like ___: 2 words
31 Revolutions ___ minute (what RPM stands for on a record)
33 Ticklish Muppet
34 Blue cartoon character
36 ___ York City
38 Use a chair
39 Jacket
41 "Now I get it!"
43 ___ Wednesday (holiday that's four days before Easter)

45 Large, dangerous reptile
50 Part of the foot
51 Where a camper sleeps
52 "Easy ___ it!" ("Be careful!")
53 Dead-___ street
54 Observes
55 Clubs, diamonds, hearts, or spades

DOWN

1 "Oh, give ___ home where the buffalo roam ...": 2 words
2 Bird that's awake at night
3 The note after fa
4 "___ to My Lou"
5 Rip into pieces: 2 words
6 Columbus Day's month: Abbreviation
7 Cut vegetables into bits
8 South ___ (country whose capital is Seoul)
9 Small animals that eat rodents
10 Possess
11 Damp
16 Chatter on and on
20 Word that begins many book titles

21 "How long ___ this been going on?"

22 Money-dispensing device at a bank: Abbreviation

23 Felt

25 Five times two

27 "How ___ supposed to know?": 2 words

28 Polka ___ (circle on a fabric)

30 Athlete who's in the big leagues

32 Jumps when someone says "Boo!," for example

35 They aren't fiction

37 "Halt! ___ goes there?"

40 Part of a forest

42 Puts two and two together

43 Nibbled on

44 Male child

46 "It's just ___ of those things"

47 It shows that you're in debt to someone

48 Colorful ring of flowers in Hawaii

49 Suffix that means "most"

9

ACROSS

1 "Four-and-twenty blackbirds baked in ___": 2 words
5 Upper limbs
9 Full-time athlete
12 What a baby might call its father
13 ___ Place (square in Monopoly)
14 George W. Bush's political party: Abbreviation
15 Brand of low-calorie cola: 2 words
17 "Now ___ seen everything!"
18 Group that sends astronauts into space: Abbreviation
19 The ___ the moon: 2 words
21 Take a bath
25 Puts frosting on a cake
26 Brand of soft drink: 2 words
30 Actors Cruise and Hanks
31 Cost an arm ___ leg: 2 words
32 Really, really fat
34 What a sled driver yells to the dogs

38 "Open 9 ___ 5" (sign on a store window)
39 Brand of ginger ale
44 Word that people yell to encourage a bullfighter
45 Wholesome
46 Small pie
47 Guinea pig or goldfish, sometimes
48 What a bird builds
49 Bills that have George Washington on them

DOWN

1 Use a plus sign
2 Ache
3 Notion
4 Munches on
5 "Tarzan, the ___ Man"
6 Queen Latifah's music
7 ___ Butterworth's (brand of syrup)
8 Kind of milk without much fat in it
9 What a frog might turn into, in a fairy tale
10 Article that says whether a movie is good or bad
11 Unwraps

16 The least important piece in chess

20 Kool-___ (fruity drink)

22 One thing ___ time: 2 words

23 ___ Diego, California

24 Concealed

26 ___ home (big trailer)

27 Food you might have at brunch

28 The ___ Enterprise ("Star Trek" spacecraft)

29 Don, John, or Ron, for example

30 From bottom ___: 2 words

33 Sports fan's favorite TV channel: Abbreviation

35 "I've had it ___ here!": 2 words

36 Have a short attention ___

37 What you say during roll call

40 ___ cards (things that have actors' lines written on them)

41 60-minute periods: Abbreviation

42 Not dry

43 Cars drive on them: Abbreviation

10

ACROSS

1 Get in the tub
6 ___ and flow (what the tide does)
9 Nut produced by an oak
10 "___ aboard!"
11 Young boy, to his parents
14 Casper is a friendly one
15 Take someone to court
16 Honest ___ (President Lincoln's nickname)
17 "Ready, ___, go!"
18 Devoured
20 Neither this ___ that
21 What a cowboy rides
23 Went to dinner and a movie with
25 Couch
27 Where the funny bone is
29 Boston's state: Abbreviation
30 Far ___ (nowhere near each other)
32 ___ training (what new soldiers go through)
34 The end of the school week: Abbreviation
35 Sharp change of direction for a driver: Hyphenated

37 Carry around
40 It might be pierced
41 ___ Francisco, California
42 Without ___ in the world (stress-free): 2 words
44 Introverted
45 Relatives
46 Baton ___ (Louisiana's capital)
47 Sneaky
48 Doesn't win

DOWN

1 What groceries are put into
2 Feel sore
3 She puts money under your pillow: 2 words
4 Periods of 3,600 seconds: Abbreviation
5 Opposite of "exit"
6 He puts eggs into your basket: 2 words
7 Color of the sky
8 Mix together
11 He puts gifts in your stocking: 2 words

12 Long, thin musical instruments

13 Geeky people

19 Quiet ___ mouse: 2 words

22 Paddle

24 "What a good boy ___!" (what Little Jack Horner said): 2 words

25 People lock money and valuables in these

26 ___ Winfrey (talk show host)

28 February follower: Abbreviation

31 An elephant has two of them

33 Growl

36 A Manx cat doesn't have one

38 Encourage

39 The Bee ___ (disco group from the 1970s)

43 Sound that a pigeon makes

11

ACROSS

1 Brag
6 Money paid to a lawyer
9 Little drink
12 Bombay and Calcutta are cities in this country
13 "You dirty ___!"
14 Card that can beat a king
15 Molars and bicuspids
16 "And so on and so forth": Abbreviation
17 Not old
18 Billboard, for example
20 Scalding
22 "Where ___ go from here?": 2 words
25 Tic-___-toe
26 Speedy
29 Breakfast food that you might put jelly on: 2 words
33 Not crazy
34 What a sunbather gets
35 Ending for "differ"
36 A little strange
38 Hold ___ (grip)
40 Pickle container
42 Deaf ___ post: 2 words
44 What elephant tusks are made of

48 In this day and ___ (currently)
49 "That's true"
50 "Long-___ varmint" (what Yosemite Sam called Bugs Bunny)
51 ___ off (start to fall asleep)
52 ___ the table (get ready for dinner)
53 Winter vehicles

DOWN

1 Little ___ (small amount)
2 Twelve minus eleven
3 It can come after "Gator" or "orange"
4 Stops standing up
5 Tropical island in the south Pacific
6 Breakfast food that you might put syrup on: 2 words
7 Swallow
8 ___ A Sketch (drawing toy)
9 Capital of New Mexico: 2 words
10 ___ cream cone
11 Long seat in a church

19 Laughing ___ (something the dentist might give you)

21 Word on a light switch

22 ___ Moines, Iowa

23 "Little Miss Muffet sat ___ tuffet ...": 2 words

24 Paid no attention to

27 "It's a ___ to tell a lie"

28 It's used to blow things up: Abbreviation

30 Was in front of everyone else

31 Fellow

32 Gets rid of knots

37 A week has seven of them

39 Egg-shaped

40 One of the kids on "The Brady Bunch"

41 Many years ___ (in the distant past)

43 "___ what I mean?"

45 Portland's state: Abbreviation

46 The color at the top of a rainbow

47 A football field is measured in these units: Abbreviation

12

ACROSS

1 Quick
5 They're higher than face cards
9 "Put on your thinking ___!"
12 Big curve, like on a McDonald's sign
13 You pour it over cereal
14 Spanish word for "one"
15 ___ and tear (day-to-day damage)
16 Prefix that means "against"
17 Nut used in Southern pies
19 Democrat's opponent: Abbreviation
21 Mother deer
22 Rock back and forth
23 Frightened feeling
24 Quit
25 Superman or Batman, for example
27 It can be "revolving" or "sliding"
29 What cows say
31 They're attached to the shoulders
33 "Wish you ___ here" (phrase on a postcard)

36 TV network that shows "Buffy the Vampire Slayer": Abbreviation
37 "Golly!"
38 Where to go bowling
39 ___ good example: 2 words
41 Male deer
43 Sara ___ (brand of frozen desserts)
44 Country in the Middle East
45 Masking ___
46 Want ___ (newspaper section where people buy and sell things)
47 All the actors in a play
48 You can ride downhill on one

DOWN

1 Bambi was one
2 "You ___ what you eat"
3 Frighten
4 Loose pieces of string
5 "Today I ___ man" (bar mitzvah boy's phrase): 2 words
6 Disney heroine
7 ___ John (pop singer)

28

8 Went down a mountain, maybe
9 They hold drinks
10 Turn over ___ leaf: 2 words
11 Disney heroine
18 How military people say "yes"
20 Athlete who isn't an amateur
23 Large tree-covered areas
26 Dusting cloth
28 A friend of Winnie-the-Pooh

29 It might be country and western or rhythm and blues
30 Soap ___ (kind of TV show)
32 Copper or iron, for example
34 Small device used by a saxophone player
35 They have lids and lashes
38 Grew older
40 Small insect
42 King Kong, for one

13

ACROSS

1 ___ the wrong way (irritate)
4 "Cat ___ your tongue?"
7 Device that police use to catch speeders
12 Mad ___ wet hen: 2 words
13 ___ de Janeiro (city in Brazil)
14 "Aida" is a famous one
15 European country
17 "___ and the Brain" (cartoon)
18 "___ me no questions and I'll tell you no lies"
19 "Things are not always what they ___"
20 Puts a worm on a fishhook
23 It takes kids to school
24 "Act your ___ and not your shoe size!"
27 Shrek is one
28 Take part in a footrace
29 Small brown bird
30 Edgar Allan ___ (famous writer)
31 Where bacon comes from
32 Jabbed with one's finger

33 ___-back (easygoing)
35 ___ Francisco, California
36 Take a long, long look
38 European country
42 Someone who has possession of something
43 Strike with one's fist
44 Perform
45 Soft drinks
46 ___ distance (far away): 2 words
47 ___ Willie Winkie

DOWN

1 Old cloth
2 "___ only as directed" (instruction on medicine)
3 ___ mitzvah (ceremony for a Jewish boy)
4 What a lawn mower cuts
5 Hog's noise
6 Plaything
7 You can make knots in them
8 "... blackbirds baked in ___": 2 words
9 European country
10 Noah built one

11 "___ of Light" (Madonna song)

16 First ___ (assistant on a ship)

19 The closest star to the Earth

20 Baby ___ (Barney's friend)

21 "A long time ___ in a galaxy far, far away ..."

22 European country

23 Insect

25 "Holy cow!"

26 Tight ___ (position in football)

28 Get ___ of (eliminate)

29 "___ you be my neighbor?" (question from Mr. Rogers)

31 Docks

32 Italian food

34 ___ code (first part of a phone number)

35 Formal wear for a man

36 Letters that mean "We're in trouble!"

37 How many things make a pair

38 "Now I understand!"

39 Not cooked

40 ___ skating

41 Had a meal

14

ACROSS

1 Suggest a price at an auction
4 "___ one in is a rotten egg!"
8 Food that's a lot like jelly
11 Game with "Wild" and "Draw Two" cards
12 Busy as ___: 2 words
13 Positive
14 Fruity candy
16 Letters after H
17 What one little piggy cried all the way home
18 Ballerina's skirt
20 Company that makes toys you build things with
23 ___ talk (speech given to a team)
24 Large
27 Give it ___ (try it): 2 words
28 "Eight ___ a-milking" ("Twelve Days of Christmas" gift)
30 Australian bird that can't fly
31 Scary sound heard on Halloween
32 Insect that lives in a hill
33 Cable channel for people who love sports: Abbreviation

34 ___ and girls
36 It might be unleaded
38 Pushed out a long breath
40 Chocolate-covered malt balls
45 Deserve
46 Monetary unit of Spain, France, Greece, and Germany
47 "Thank ___"
48 They are used to sell things to people
49 A clarinet player uses one
50 Lamb's mother

DOWN

1 "The Magic School ___" (cartoon show)
2 It's inside a pen
3 "What ___ know?": 2 words
4 Not early
5 Ready, willing, and ___
6 "___ you later, alligator!"
7 Gave a quiz
8 Fruit-flavored candy
9 Noah's ___
10 ___ Gibson (actor in the "Lethal Weapon" movies)
13 Fill a chair

15 Number of singers in a duet

19 ___ and downs

20 Where a scientist works

21 A vain person may have a big one

22 Chocolate-covered peanuts

23 The hard center of a peach

25 Mischievous kid

26 Weapon that uses bullets

28 It comes before June

29 Solution

33 The "sixth sense," supposedly

35 "Mind your ___ business!"

36 He was Clinton's vice president

37 Like two peas in ___: 2 words

38 "Well, I'll ___ monkey's uncle!": 2 words

39 What a Scottish person calls a young man

41 Shade of color

42 Word before "lash" or "lid"

43 Move a canoe through the water

44 "So ___ me!" (sarcastic remark)

15

ACROSS

1 Not slow
5 "___ Ran the Zoo" (Dr. Seuss book): 2 words
8 ___ Albert (1970s cartoon character)
11 It gets wrinkles out of clothes
12 Skinny
13 Words at a wedding: 2 words
14 Fuzz that comes from clothing
15 ___ a living (bring home a paycheck)
16 Character in "Winnie-the-Pooh"
17 What a tourist to Hawaii wears as a necklace
18 Odds and ___ (various things)
19 Really annoying person
20 Find fault with
22 Swap
24 Make ___ of (put to work)
25 Animal that gives milk
26 It comes out of a faucet
28 Person who comes in last place
31 Marries
32 ___ tire (driving problem)
34 Large barrel
36 "Mary ___ a little lamb"
37 Body parts that have nails
38 It shows everything a restaurant serves
39 Adam's wife, in the Bible
40 One of the friends on "Friends"
41 Suggest strongly
42 Todd and Rod Flanders's dad, on "The Simpsons"
43 "___ a Small World After All"
44 They change things' colors

DOWN

1 ___ in the blanks
2 The sign of the Ram, in the zodiac
3 Hedgehog in video games
4 Explosive stuff: Abbreviation
5 "___ no idea!" ("You're kidding!"): 2 words

6 Level of Boy Scouts: 2 words

7 Holiday ___ (hotel chain)

8 "You're ___!" (what a boss might say to a bad employee)

9 Love a lot

10 Grabbed

12 Level of Boy Scouts

18 "What ___ is new?"

19 Horror movie about a vicious shark

21 A baseball team gets three of them per inning

23 ___ beer (flavor of soda)

26 Make cloth

27 Did some math

29 "___ cloud has a silver lining"

30 "Home on the ___"

31 "At what time?"

33 Not as much

35 Monday follower: Abbreviation

37 Prefix that means "three"

38 Pigs wallow in it

16

ACROSS

1 Dogs walk on them
5 You can catch a mouse in one
9 Sack
12 State where the 2002 Winter Olympics were held
13 Person who fights the villain
14 Open ___ can of worms: 2 words
15 Dorothy's dog in "The Wizard of Oz"
16 Go to ___ (go too far)
18 "And more": Abbreviation
20 Noisy kind of dancing
21 The normal score, on a golf course
23 Blind as ___: 2 words
27 Actual
30 Suffix that can follow "lion"
31 Its capital is Austin
33 What a hitter sometimes tries to get, in baseball: Abbreviation
34 ___ monster (reptile in the Southwest)
36 Where the throat is
37 You sleep in it
38 "___ no big deal"
40 What people say when they get married: 2 words
42 Where people stroll next to a road
47 Compass direction
50 "___ Ventura, Pet Detective"
51 "I cannot tell ___": 2 words
52 Part of a constellation
53 Positive response
54 Feel sorry for
55 Game where you see things "with my little eye": 2 words

DOWN

1 "Don't ___ all your eggs in one basket"
2 From ___ Z (completely): 2 words
3 You'll get wet while having fun on them in the summer: 2 words
4 What a doctor gives you with a needle
5 On ___ nose (exactly)
6 Tyrannosaurus ___
7 It's found in museums
8 Where ships go in and out
9 You'll get wet while having fun on them in the summer: 2 words
10 Relative of a chimpanzee

11 It makes cars go

17 "In one ___ and out the other"

19 Black ___ (animal that's considered unlucky)

21 It's used to hold a tent in place

22 "Just ___ suspected!": 2 words

24 Big ___ (famous landmark in London)

25 Tool for chopping wood

26 Tic-___-toe

28 President Lincoln's nickname

29 Covering of the eye

32 ___ resort (place for some winter vacationers)

35 Had supper

39 Trade

41 ___ Arnaz (star of "I Love Lucy")

42 "You can ___ that again!"

43 Skating on thin ___ (in a risky situation)

44 "Prince ___" (song in "Aladdin")

45 Started a fire

46 Lock opener

48 Syrup is made out of this

49 Do one's best

ACROSS

1 What Babe was, in the movie "Babe"
4 Food used in an omelet
7 Not the present or future
11 "Just who do you think you ___?"
12 Amount of bread
14 General Robert ___: 2 words
15 ___ bull terrier (kind of dog)
16 Pout
17 The bottom of the foot
18 Houston baseball team
20 It follows summer
22 "Beat it!"
23 Make, as a salary
25 Groundhog ___ (February 2)
26 Watch young kids while their parents are away: Hyphenated
29 Brother's sibling, for short
32 Song for two people
33 Slippery ___ eel: 2 words
37 National ___ (patriotic song)

39 Fudge ___ (ice cream flavor)
41 "Hey, what's the big ___?"
42 Someone who writes rhymes
44 In a ___ (one after another)
45 Fibber
46 Brings to trial
47 Insect that loves picnics
48 Identical
49 Pigpen
50 Word of agreement

DOWN

1 Fathers
2 From Dublin
3 "___ the point!" ("Stop stalling!"): 2 words
4 Tickle Me ___ (stuffed toy)
5 Series of horror books by R.L. Stine
6 Empty space between two teeth
7 Nuisance
8 Read ___ (say the words on the page)

1	2	3	■	4	5	6	■	7	8	9	10
11			■	12		13	■	14			
15			■	16			■	17			
18		19		■	20	21			■		
22				■	23	24			■	25	
■	■	26	27				■	28		■	■
29	30	31	■	32			■	33	34	35	36
37			38		■	39	40		■		
41			■	42	43		■	44			
45			■	46			■	47			
48			■	49			■	50			

9 Patty and ___ (Marge Simpson's sisters)

10 ___-weeny

13 Series of horror books by R.L. Stine: 2 words

19 Steal from

21 Prefix that means "one"

24 How soldiers say "yes"

27 Suffix for "lemon" or "Gator"

28 ___ water (what comes out of a faucet)

29 Big triangular pieces of cloth on a boat

30 Country where Calcutta and Bombay are

31 What a teakettle gives off

34 Use an aerosol can

35 By oneself

36 Colorful salamanders

38 Animal similar to a rabbit

40 "The ___-Bitsy Spider"

43 Ending for "danger" or "outrage"

18

ACROSS

1 Scorching
4 The Liberty ___ (Philadelphia attraction)
8 "An apple ___ keeps the doctor away": 2 words
12 Your and my
13 Place
14 What a dog likes to chew on
15 School group: Abbreviation
16 Young pets: 2 words
18 Word in the middle square of a bingo card
20 "For ___ a jolly good fellow ..."
21 More secure
23 Soaking ___
24 Police officer
27 Liquid that's inside batteries
28 Means of transportation
29 ___ fish sandwich
30 Christmas's month: Abbreviation
31 "It's really cold!"
32 The lesson at the end of a fable
33 "Curly ___" (kids' movie from 1991)
34 Points a camera
35 Young pets: 2 words

39 "A mind ___ terrible thing to waste": 2 words
42 China's continent
43 "Sure, sure!": 2 words
44 Moving ___ (kind of truck)
45 Desire
46 Neat
47 From beginning to ___ (completely)

DOWN

1 Move like a rabbit
2 "___ of the frying pan, into the fire"
3 ___ jam (lots of drivers in one place)
4 Someone who makes bread
5 One of the Great Lakes
6 Allow
7 Foam
8 The alphabet
9 "___ good turn daily" (Boy Scout slogan): 2 words
10 Insect that builds colonies
11 What the Spanish word "sí" means in English
17 Not ___ (not so far)

19 Scarlet
21 Unhappy
22 High card
23 The Revolutionary ___ (period of U.S. history)
24 Kind of writing that isn't printing
25 Put ___ show (entertain people): 2 words
26 Good friend
28 ___ card (alternative to checks or cash)
29 "The piper's son," in a nursery rhyme
31 Purchase

32 A little foggy
33 Small fight
34 Became older
35 What a dog holds up if you teach it to "shake"
36 Its capital is Washington, D.C.: Abbreviation
37 ___ the tail on the donkey
38 ___-Wan Kenobi (character in "Star Wars")
40 ___ Antonio, Texas
41 This ___ that

19

ACROSS

1 Containers that could be made of paper or plastic
5 "Don't cry ___ spilled milk"
9 Plenty: 2 words
10 Half of ten
11 "___ la la" (sounds in a song)
14 ___ pad (what a frog might sit on)
15 "Do not ___ the animals" (sign at the zoo)
16 Like summertime weather
17 Was ahead of the other competitors
18 When the sun comes up
19 Formal dance for high-school students
20 "Have a ___ day!"
22 "Sesame ___" (Big Bird's show)
24 ___ and found department
26 Stick out like a ___ thumb (be obvious)
27 Took a peek
29 Island country ruled by Fidel Castro
31 Insect that could bother a dog
32 Board game where you try to conquer the whole world
34 Ending for "north" or "south"
36 Poison ___ (plant that could give you a rash)
37 Country whose capital is Teheran
38 On ___ (marked down from the full price)
39 Wife's title: Abbreviation
40 Something you aren't supposed to do: Hyphenated
41 All the sailors on a ship
42 What Sebastian was, in "The Little Mermaid"
43 "Well, ___ that special!"

DOWN

1 Many sports are played with one
2 Someone who comes from another planet
3 Heroine of a fairy tale
4 Where pigs live
5 "Take a long walk ___ short pier!": 2 words
6 What tourists like to have from their hotel windows

42

7 Happenings

8 Tomato's color

11 They discovered 3-Down in their house: 2 words

12 "Money is the ___ of all evil"

13 Bank device where people get cash: Abbreviation

18 Furniture in a classroom

19 Country in South America

21 Make a meal

23 ___, paper, scissors (game played with hands)

25 Severe fright

27 Someone you can't trust

28 ___ Prince (Wonder Woman's secret identity)

30 City where the cartoon "King of the Hill" takes place

31 ___ Sawyer (boy in a Mark Twain book)

33 Someone who looks down on other people

35 Amphibian with a long tail

37 "Monsters, ___" (2001 film)

38 ___-fi (kind of fiction)

20

ACROSS

1 Not to mention
5 Classified ___ (newspaper section)
8 Divisions of a play
12 Lug around
13 "Don't ___ on it!" ("It isn't likely")
14 In this place
15 "___ the Rainbow" (song from "The Wizard of Oz")
16 Hole-in-___ (golfer's goal)
17 Prayer ending
18 "The Princess and the ___" (fairy tale)
19 Opposite of inner
21 "___ your heart out!"
22 Intelligent
24 What an artist uses
26 Get ___ of (dispose of)
27 Stuff that blows up: Abbreviation
28 Centers of apples
30 Groups of players
32 Buddy
33 Marathons and sprints
35 "For what ___ worth ..."
37 Flower seen at Easter
39 Food fish
40 Door that you leave through
41 Region
42 Child
43 Boy's name that sounds the same as the girl's name "Jean"
44 New ___ City
45 ___ as a fox
46 Got bigger

DOWN

1 Spinning like ___: 2 words
2 More than likes
3 Big vehicle used by construction workers
4 "___ the ramparts we watched ..." (lyric in "The Star-Spangled Banner")
5 Nothing to write home ___
6 Bump in a car's fender
7 Hard to climb
8 "So that's it!"
9 Big vehicle used by construction workers: 2 words

10 "Trick or ___!"

11 Mailed off

19 Out of ___ (not where it belongs)

20 Ranks

23 "___ Bud" (movie about a basketball-playing dog)

25 ___ rush (hurrying along): 2 words

28 Capital of Egypt

29 Bags

30 ___ bear (stuffed animal)

31 R.L. ___ (author of the "Goosebumps" books)

32 "All work and no ___ makes Jack a dull boy"

34 Loop of rope

36 Food that contains meat and vegetables

38 Large, hairy animal from Asia

40 What a chicken lays

21

ACROSS

1 Line where fabric is stitched together

5 "What have ___ to lose?": 2 words

9 Pokémon trainer's name

12 Spider-Man is one

13 Ripped

14 "What ___ care?" ("No difference to me!"): 2 words

15 Needles, potatoes, and faces all have them

16 Have ___ in your bonnet (have crazy ideas): 2 words

17 ___ and crafts

19 What horses eat

21 Ending for "lion"

22 Rocks falling from the sky

24 "This ___ man, he played one ..."

26 Triangle or rectangle, for example

27 Women who clean houses

29 Suffix for "Japan"

30 Luggage that you take with you into an airplane: Hyphenated

32 ___ Vegas, Nevada

34 When many people eat lunch

36 "___ to leap tall buildings in a single bound" (description of Superman)

37 "___ Mommy Kissing Santa Claus": 2 words

39 Person who lives in the Middle East, perhaps

41 "Definitely!"

42 You need five of them to play Yahtzee

43 Brand of spaghetti sauce

44 It's more than "-er"

45 "For Pete's ___!"

46 Toboggan

DOWN

1 That lady

2 Depressed friend of Winnie-the-Pooh

3 Locations

4 Opposite of least

5 Give ___ shot (try): 2 words

6 Lie down at night: 2 words, 1 of them hyphenated

7 Rocks that contain valuable metals

8 Golfers' pegs

9 ___ and Eve (first two people in the Bible)

10 Tender spots on one's skin

11 Lie down at night: 3 words

18 Sail the seven ___ (travel the whole world)

20 Fly like an eagle

23 "___ sesame!" (Ali Baba's magic words)

25 Money that was used in Italy until 2002

27 "It won't be easy, but I'll ___ somehow"

28 Shoe bottoms

30 What ocean reefs are made from

31 Bird's home

32 Jar tops

33 Afghanistan is on this continent

35 Rowing tools

38 Like Willie Winkie

40 It opens to become a flower

22

ACROSS

1 Jet ___ (problem for someone who flies a long way)
4 ___ gun (toy weapon)
7 U-___ (company that rents moving vans)
11 Ending for "Vietnam" or "Siam"
12 "___ not like green eggs and ham!": 2 words
13 Furthermore
14 They could be told at slumber parties: 2 words
17 X-___ vision (one of Superman's powers)
18 Cat that chased Jerry, in cartoons
19 Like really loose pants
22 ___ up (make more lively)
23 What a sheep says
26 "... blackbirds baked in ___": 2 words
27 Partner of "neither"
28 Be entitled to
29 One plus two plus three plus four
30 ___ and reel (fishing equipment)
31 Gave a job to
32 What people breathe

33 Someone might drink coffee out of it
34 They could happen at slumber parties: 2 words
40 Shape of a racetrack
41 "___ in apple": 2 words
42 Iced ___ (cool drink)
43 Church seats
44 Twelve-month periods: Abbreviation
45 To this point

DOWN

1 Chicken drumstick
2 Stuff at the bottom of a fireplace
3 First name of presidents Washington and Bush
4 Oklahoma ___
5 "Help wanted" notices
6 "Harry ___ and the Sorcerer's Stone"
7 Hurt
8 Aladdin pretended to be this prince, in the movie
9 "___ your head!" ("Don't be stupid!")
10 ___ Angeles, California
15 Before you can ___ Jack Robinson (very quickly)

16 "Alley ___" (old comic about a caveman)

19 Animal that hangs upside-down in a cave

20 Orangutan

21 What you say when you win a certain card game

22 Pea holder

23 Salad ___ (place to make your own salad)

24 "Your eyes ___ bigger than your stomach"

25 What the symbol "&" means

27 Country next to Sweden

28 100 minus 20

30 ___ de Janeiro, Brazil

31 Embrace

32 "___ well that ends well"

33 Little ___ Muffet

34 "___! Goes the Weasel"

35 "___ Been Working on the Railroad"

36 Break the ___ (do something illegal)

37 Opposite of near

38 A golfer puts a ball on one

39 Got into a chair

23

ACROSS

1 Search high and ___ (look everywhere)
4 Well-defended places for troops to stay
9 Not many
12 ___ trance (hypnotized): 2 words
13 Tornado ___ (weather warning)
14 "___ got an idea"
15 ___ peeve (something you especially dislike)
16 Newspapers, television, radio, etc.
17 Mr. Flanders, on "The Simpsons"
18 Lamb's mommy
20 "Wild horses couldn't ___ it out of me"
22 Make well
24 Spelling ___
26 Grouchy
29 ___ in a while (occasionally)
30 Moved quickly
31 Craving
32 "Tiny ___ Adventures"
33 State-of-the-___ (like new technology)
34 "X marks the ___"
35 Wildcat with a short tail
37 Split-___ soup

38 Flying saucer: Abbreviation
40 Long-time maker of video games
43 "___ the Great Pumpkin, Charlie Brown"
46 Miles ___ gallon (what "mpg" means)
47 Entered a car: 2 words
48 "Ready or ___, here I come!"
49 What the messages are in the TV announcement "We'll be right back after these messages"
50 Some of the sounds in Rice Krispies
51 "___ Story" (movie about Buzz Lightyear and Woody)

DOWN

1 Part of the mouth
2 Half of two
3 You can make pictures with them
4 ___ and fortune (what celebrities have)
5 It's shouted at a bullfight
6 Fire truck's color
7 Brand of sugarless gum

50

8 It might be on top of a Christmas tree

9 You can make pictures with it: 2 words

10 The first woman, in the Bible

11 Marry

19 Teeny-___

21 Entertain

22 Simple bed for a camper

23 Spanish for 2-Down

24 Toni ___ ("Un-Break My Heart" singer)

25 ___, nose, and throat (specialty of some doctors)

27 Long ___ (not recently)

28 You need one to play badminton

36 Constantly gets on one's case

37 Bowling balls hit them

38 Put ___ brave front (pretend not to be scared): 2 words

39 Gave a meal to

41 ___ moment's notice (with no warning): 2 words

42 Tear

44 ___ close for comfort

45 Place for pigs

24

ACROSS

1 People form them when they sit down
5 Thick cups
9 Weather that makes it hard to see
12 Opposite of entrance
13 Big, bushy hairstyle
14 "Let sleeping dogs ___"
15 TV's "warrior princess"
16 Wacky person
18 Boast
20 "That's the ___ the cookie crumbles!"
21 Cool ___ cucumber: 2 words
23 Bone inside your chest
25 Group of long, skinny fish
29 Guy's date
30 Big meal
33 "___ said it!"
34 Message-carrying birds in the Harry Potter books
36 One thing ___ time (not all together): 2 words
37 Female animal on a farm
38 It says "You've got mail!" on the computer: Abbreviation
41 Person from Iran or Iraq, perhaps

43 It might be served with spaghetti
47 ___ Revere (early American hero)
50 Plant that climbs up walls
51 Like the Devil
52 "What ___ can I say?"
53 "Monkey ___, monkey do"
54 Shrill barks from dogs
55 You can go down a snowy hill on one

DOWN

1 ___ Luthor (Superman's archenemy)
2 Tool that's like a big hatchet
3 Game with flippers, bumpers, and a plunger
4 Five-pointed shape
5 The baby on "The Simpsons"
6 Mysterious vision in the sky: Abbreviation
7 Enlarge
8 Living room furniture
9 Miami's state: Abbreviation
10 Black fuel

11 Stuff that can make hair stay in place

17 "See you later!"

19 What Little Orphan Annie's dog says

21 In the past

22 Tool that can come after "chain" or "hack"

24 Statement from a sheep

26 Round thing in the front of your head

27 Near the ground

28 One of the ghosts in Ms. Pac-Man

31 Tries to gain some extra time

32 Sticky stuff used to make roads

35 Part of the weekend: Abbreviation

39 Follow orders

40 It comes out of a volcano

42 "Planet of the ___"

43 Prefix for "behave" or "spell"

44 Mother of Cain and Abel

45 How Marines say "yes"

46 "Button your ___" ("Be quiet")

48 Put to good ___ (take advantage of)

49 Was in first place

25

ACROSS

1 Discussion
5 "___ sells seashells down by the seashore"
8 First ___ (captain's assistant on a boat)
12 "He isn't ___ to see the forest for the trees"
13 Fuel that people drill for
14 "Shake ___!" ("Hurry up!"): 2 words
15 Fun activity that takes place at a rink: 2 words
18 Opposite of longitude, on a map: Abbreviation
19 ___ down (stop standing up)
20 Couch potatoes watch them: Abbreviation
23 Toy that spins
25 What an Olympic athlete tries to win
29 Cards that twos might go on top of, in solitaire
31 Like Garfield the cat
33 Part of an ear that gets pierced
34 Terrific
36 It comes before Thursday: Abbreviation
38 "___ a life!"
39 "___, Virginia, there is a Santa Claus"
41 Burned ___ crisp: 2 words

43 Fun activity that takes place at an 18-hole course: 2 words
50 "It hit me like ___ of bricks": 2 words
51 "Just ___ thought!": 2 words
52 Great Lake that Cleveland is next to
53 ___ a bell (sounded familiar)
54 It makes vehicles run
55 What grows into a plant

DOWN

1 Convertible or compact, for example
2 Cable channel that people pay extra for: Abbreviation
3 ___ of a sudden (without warning)
4 "___ me about it!"
5 In a way: 2 words
6 ___ and hers
7 Animals related to moose
8 Company that makes Barbie dolls
9 Muhammad ___
10 Number of this clue
11 Silly Putty container
16 Have brunch

17 Point a bow and arrow
20 Game where people try to avoid being "it"
21 You can watch movies at home on it: Abbreviation
22 "Long time no ___!"
24 Cat's hand
26 Grown-up puppy
27 Lincoln's nickname
28 ___ the cat out of the bag (tell a secret)
30 Familiar quotation
32 Computer game involving falling shapes
35 Drink that's very popular in China
37 Mother of a fawn

40 Father of a fawn
42 The Middle ___ (period of history about 1000 years ago)
43 Month after February: Abbreviation
44 Give ___ whirl (try): 2 words
45 Prefix for "sense" or "profit"
46 Country that became independent in 1776: Abbreviation
47 State that's north of California: Abbreviation
48 Say something untrue
49 Made a meal for

26

ACROSS

1 Large, horned river animal
6 To and ___ (in both directions)
9 That woman
12 "Make no mistake ___ it"
13 Struck a match
14 "___ you!" (shout to get someone's attention)
15 U.S tourist site featuring carved faces of presidents: 2 words
18 The Mediterranean ___
19 "___ off the grass" (sign in some yards)
20 Huge
23 Get ___ of (remove)
25 Very fast
28 Where the Great Salt Lake is
30 Piece of wood that goes in a fireplace
32 Jay ___ (host of "The Tonight Show")
33 Gave a challenge to
35 Run out of ___ (lose energy)
37 Small rodent
38 Made pictures
40 At this moment
42 U.S. tourist site featuring lots of swamps and forests: 2 words
48 Was in a race
49 "___ got it!"
50 Fruit that can be black or green
51 "___ a miracle!"
52 Had followers
53 Winter weather

DOWN

1 What Aries is, in the zodiac
2 Cable channel that shows lots of movies: Abbreviation
3 Paper that describes a debt
4 Some religious women
5 Playful river animal
6 Virus that many people get in the winter
7 Board game that shows a map of the world
8 In one ear and out the ___
9 Someone who goes out to buy things
10 Not him
11 Private ___ (detective)
16 What you can hold onto when climbing stairs
17 Breakfast or dinner, for example

20 What a small flower is before it blooms

21 Call ___ day (quit for now): 2 words

22 Places to grow vegetables or flowers

24 Dalmatian or dachshund

26 "Rub-a-dub-dub, three men ___ tub ...": 2 words

27 Small circle

29 "Take this"

31 Kool and the ___ (music group)

34 Person with horns and a pitchfork

36 Songs that are sung by just one person

39 "___ been through a lot together ..."

41 Humpty Dumpty sat on one

42 Prefix for "pod" or "cycle"

43 A magician might pull a rabbit out of one

44 Bright color

45 Opposite of "live"

46 The night before a holiday, like Christmas

47 TV ___

ACROSS

1 Not skinny
4 Opposite of "fail"
8 Country next to Iraq
12 Grampa's real first name, on "The Simpsons"
13 Laugh ___ (something very funny)
14 What a fisherman uses to get a fish's attention
15 Certain baseball player: 2 words
18 "... or ___!" (end of a threat)
19 What a beach is made of
20 "I'm at my wit's ___!"
21 Doze
23 Travel on snow, in a way
24 Word that can come after "X" or "sting"
25 Boat that travels underwater, for short
27 Home for a hog
29 Wynken, Blynken, and ___ (people in a nursery rhyme)
32 Baby
34 Capital of Oregon
38 Jungle animal
39 Verbal
41 Capital of Peru

42 Player near the shortstop: 2 words
45 What breakfast in bed is served on
46 Red "Sesame Street" Muppet
47 Participate in an auction
48 How a Southerner might say "you"
49 Rod and ___ (things used in fishing)
50 Sneaky, like a fox

DOWN

1 Clocks and people have them
2 "That rings ___" ("It sounds familiar"): 2 words
3 Stressed out
4 It can come before "school" or "teen"
5 Puts on TV
6 Pieces of living room furniture
7 Smells bad
8 Sick
9 Less polite
10 Sports stadium

1	2	3		4	5	6	7		8	9	10	11
12				13					14			
15			16				17					
18					19					20		
21			22		23				24			
		25		26		27		28				
29	30	31		32		33		34		35	36	37
38				39			40		41			
42			43				44					
45					46				47			
48					49				50			

11 Like a geek

16 Golf balls rest on them

17 Works at a newspaper, maybe

22 "___ a happy face": 2 words

26 The dividing point between two states

28 College that's a rival of Harvard

29 Disgusting

30 Kind of music where people might sing in Italian

31 Stick-on design

33 ___ of contents (part of a book)

35 Arms and legs, for example

36 Some of it is spam: Hyphenated

37 ___ Moore (pop singer)

40 Like a really unconvincing excuse

43 Olive ___ (Popeye's girlfriend)

44 The note that comes before la

ACROSS

1 Frilly white fabric
5 "Lord of the ___" (nickname for Tarzan)
9 Look ___ (visit): 2 words
10 Home for bats
11 Small animal with whiskers
14 Dweeb
15 Pine or poplar
16 Ginger ___
17 Family room
18 Raw metal
19 Grin
21 Former TV alien from Melmac who liked to eat cats
22 Gets married to
24 "A ___ apple": 2 words
25 Part of a camera
27 Transportation from the airport, sometimes
29 Say grace, for example
31 Turned around
33 Catch
36 The Great ___ (five bodies of water)
38 Opposite of subtract
39 "It's freezing!"

40 The best card in the game war
41 "Saturday Night ___" (TV show)
43 ___ code
44 "Uh-huh"
45 What Hansel and Gretel pushed the witch into
46 "___ in there!" ("Don't give up!")
47 Greatest
48 Have ___ in your pants (be impatient)

DOWN

1 ___ Ronstadt (famous singer)
2 Slippery as ___: 2 words
3 Kind of cereal: 2 words
4 See the light at the ___ of the tunnel
5 Julia Roberts is a famous one
6 Peeled a fruit
7 Christmas ___ (December 24)
8 Notices

11 Kind of breakfast cereal: 2 words

12 "___ Want for Christmas Is My Two Front Teeth": 2 words

13 Someone between 12 and 20

18 "Pick on somebody your ___ size!"

20 Dog in "The Grinch Who Stole Christmas"

23 Someone who goes to school

26 "You're the apple of my ___"

28 Jack ___ Jill

29 Enjoy recess

30 Three-legged ___ (picnic activity)

32 Makes a road

34 "You ___ my friend anymore!"

35 Is egotistical, in a way

37 Messy person

42 "___ been thinking ..."

43 "Now I see!"

29

ACROSS

1 "Eureka!"
4 Shoplift
7 "Jack ___ could eat no fat ..."
12 Not high
13 "___ never been so insulted in all my life!"
14 ___ bear (animal from Australia)
15 Beast from the jungle
16 Great
18 Opposite of buy
20 Gulped down
21 Russell ___ (star of "Gladiator")
23 Dessert that has a crust
24 Gentle ___ lamb: 2 words
27 Curved roof
28 Its capital is Dover: Abbreviation
29 Filthy air
30 Keep an ___ on (watch)
31 Moist
32 "___ porridge hot ..." (start of a nursery rhyme)
33 "Are you a man ___ mouse?": 2 words
34 Cameron ___ (famous actress)
35 Great
39 "Give ___ rest!" ("Enough already!"): 2 words
42 "Last ___ is a rotten egg!": 2 words
43 End of some drink names
44 Word that goes with "neither"
45 Walks in shallow water
46 The main color of a stop sign
47 "You've ___ a Friend in Me" (song from "Toy Story")

DOWN

1 Pie ___ mode: 2 words
2 "___ to it!" ("Get moving!")
3 Great
4 Long gun
5 Shaped like an egg
6 ___ Franklin (early American inventor, for short)
7 What you do at a roller rink
8 Prepare to have your picture taken
9 Animal in "Charlotte's Web"
10 "___ Baba and the Forty Thieves"

11 Tic ___ (brand of breath mints)

17 Pin the ___ on the donkey

19 Barnyard female

21 Letters between B and F

22 ___ Rogers (old-time cowboy)

23 ___ shop (where to buy a puppy)

24 Great

25 "Help us!"

26 Ice ___ (time when glaciers covered the Earth)

28 First word in a letter, often

29 Large body of water

31 Small brown birds

32 Stacked up

33 Dog that lives with Garfield

34 Guy

35 "That's incredible!"

36 "... riding ___ pony" ("Yankee Doodle" line: 2 words

37 ___ Flanders (character on "The Simpsons")

38 "So ___, so good"

40 "___ many cooks spoil the broth"

41 Stuff in museums

30

ACROSS

1 Unit of measure for land
5 "I'm ___ kidding!"
8 Beginning of the alphabet
11 ___ and pains
12 Once ___ while (sometimes): 2 words
13 It bothered a princess in a fairy tale
14 All-female group that sang "Wannabe": 3 words
17 ___ Valuable Player (sports award)
18 ___ Moines (city in the Midwest)
19 Young horse
20 Letters used during an emergency
21 Miles ___ hour
22 Glass sections of a window
23 Sheep's sound
24 Marcia and Cindy's sister on "The Brady Bunch"
25 More sensible
28 The ___ Hatter ("Alice in Wonderland" character)
29 Lifesaving technique that lifeguards need to know: Abbreviation
32 Spoken
33 Carpenter's tool
34 "Scat!"
35 All-female group that sang "Say My Name": 2 words
38 Fire ___ (stinging insect)
39 Corn could be on it
40 Parts of a skeleton
41 "You don't ___!" ("No kidding!")
42 Ram's mate, on a farm
43 They're smaller than oceans

DOWN

1 Sound of a sneeze
2 Game with kings, bishops, and pawns
3 Sleep
4 Mind-reader's ability, for short
5 More pleasant
6 The white bills in Monopoly
7 Game where you try to stay away from "It"
8 What a cook wears around the waist
9 The girl in "Beauty and the Beast"

Across / Down clues:

10 They're put on broken bones

11 Cash dispensers at banks: Abbreviation

15 An inventor starts with one

16 "I think ___" (what the Little Engine That Could said): 2 words

21 Typical score on a hole of golf

22 Scratch ___ (paper to doodle on)

23 It holds pants up

24 Horror movie about a shark

25 Fizzy drinks

26 Place for a sports event

27 Icky

28 Perhaps

29 The country that has the most people

30 Totem ___ (symbols for tribes)

31 Fishing sticks

33 What igloos are made of

34 "There was an old woman who lived in a ___ ..."

36 ___ cream sandwich

37 Network that shows "Survivor": Abbreviation

31

ACROSS

1 Action figure with a "kung fu grip": 2 words
6 Stomach muscles, for short
9 Character on "Rugrats"
12 Reversal of direction by a driver: Hyphenated
13 Glop
14 "___ good turn deserves another"
15 Made an animal less wild
16 Have
17 Fast-paced card game
18 Limerick, for example
20 Tree branch
22 "Who ___ kidding?": 2 words
24 What beavers build in a river
26 Red, white, or blue
29 Mailed
31 "What's up, ___?" (Bugs Bunny's question)
33 "___ off to see the Wizard ..."
34 Someone with a halo
36 ___-Man (old video game)
38 Where lions live
39 Bad weather for a picnic
41 Brand of spaghetti sauce
43 Kind of athlete
45 Big crowd
47 Down ___ dumps (sad): 2 words
50 Eminem's style of music
51 "I'm ___ roll!" ("Nothing is going wrong!"): 2 words
52 Person in the Indianapolis 500
53 Body part that contains the retina and cornea
54 All ___ (ready to go)
55 "On the ___ hand ..."

DOWN

1 Belly
2 Give ___ try: 2 words
3 Recess activity involving one long cord: 2 words
4 Cookie with a white cream filling
5 Finished
6 Long ___ (way back when)
7 What you eat cereal out of
8 ___ the Hedgehog
9 Recess activity involving two long cords: 2 words
10 Ramada ___ (chain of hotels)

11 Sign of the zodiac
19 Magazine that features "Spy vs. Spy"
21 Cut the grass
22 Light ___ feather: 2 words
23 Word on some rest room doors
25 Something a janitor uses
27 State on the West Coast: Abbreviation
28 ___ and Stimpy (cartoon pair)
30 Drink made by Lipton and Tetley

32 Station wagon or convertible, for example
35 Long, fancy automobiles
37 Egypt's capital
40 "That's ___ of your business!"
42 Small, annoying insect
43 Before: Prefix
44 Beam of sunshine
46 Halloween animal
48 Tee-___ (sound of a giggle)
49 "To ___ is human, to forgive divine"

ACROSS

1 Scientist's room
4 ___-friendly (easy to learn, like computers)
8 "... I met ___ with seven wives": 2 words
12 Sharp ___ tack: 2 words
13 Make a street
14 He ran against Bush in the 2000 presidential election
15 "Charlotte's ___"
16 "That woman is," as a contraction
17 Needs to pay money back to
18 Simon ___ (kids' game)
20 Exterminators kill them
22 Shut-___ (people who can't leave their rooms)
23 Casual clothing that's sometimes worn with shorts: Hyphenated
25 Gasp
27 State that borders Illinois and Missouri
28 Performed in a choir
29 "Leave ___ me!": 2 words
30 Desert animals
32 Material that can explode: Abbreviation
33 Unpopular person

35 Unit of electricity
37 "What ___ on my summer vacation" (school paper topic, sometimes): 2 words
39 Bombs that don't go off
41 "Where there's a will, there's a ___"
42 Tree with cones and needles
43 "I have no ___" ("Beats me")
44 Little bite
45 Droops
46 ___ of endearment (word like "sweetie" or "honey")
47 ___-Cone (icy dessert)

DOWN

1 Criminals break them
2 "Have ___" ("Make yourself comfortable"): 2 words
3 One way a kid can make money: Hyphenated
4 Stick-___ (bank robberies)
5 The largest desert in the world
6 Important happening

7 Take it easy
8 Many years ___
9 One way a kid can make money: 2 words
10 "___ you ashamed of yourself?"
11 The Loch ___ Monster
19 Used a BB gun
21 Unwanted e-mail
24 Happy cry after a game: 2 words
26 "That's ___ one on me" ("I've never seen that before"): 2 words

28 More depressed
29 Country whose capital is New Delhi
30 Impolite and disgusting
31 Dirty mark
32 Money left for waiters
34 Work at a magazine, perhaps
36 Printed misspelling
38 ___ Moines
40 The butcher on "The Brady Bunch"

33

ACROSS

1 Uses a question mark
5 "You can't teach an ___ dog new tricks"
8 Mary-___ Olsen ("Full House" actress, with her twin sister, Ashley)
12 "The Cosby Show" son
13 Neither here ___ there
14 Tons: 2 words
15 New York baseball team
16 "Patience ___ virtue": 2 words
17 One of the metals used to make brass
18 State next to Wyoming: Abbreviation
20 "A bird in the hand is worth ___ in the bush"
22 Pokémon trainer
24 ___ jiffy (quickly): 2 words
26 Places to live
30 Manjula's husband, on "The Simpsons"
31 Pet dog on "The Jetsons"
33 "That's disgusting!"
34 Bouncing off the walls
36 Electric ___ (kind of fish)
37 Kind of sauce used on Chinese food
38 Amount in a recipe: Abbreviation

40 Went away
42 "Gone ___ the Wind"
45 "How ___ doing?": 2 words
47 Huckleberry Finn traveled on one
50 Dog in "Garfield"
51 ___ Vegas
52 Great Lake that borders Pennsylvania
53 "The First ___" (Christmas carol)
54 Abbreviation on a speed limit sign
55 On the cutting ___ (very modern)

DOWN

1 Device at many banks: Abbreviation
2 That female
3 Red stuff you put on a hot dog
4 Just OK, not great: Hyphenated
5 White stuff you put on a hot dog
6 ___ Angeles
7 "Darn!"
8 Noisy instrument you hum into

9 ___ Baba
10 2000 pounds
11 "And so forth": Abbreviation
19 They don't tell the truth
21 Entire
22 Ooh and ___ (sound impressed)
23 "Harriet the ___" (book by Louise Fitzhugh)
25 Scarfed down
27 Yellow stuff you put on a hot dog
28 A self-centered person has a big one

29 Timid
32 Green stuff you put on a hot dog
35 Fred's wife on "I Love Lucy"
39 The front of the hand
41 At no cost
42 Was the champion
43 Wedding phrase: 2 words
44 Make a knot
46 You could use one in a treasure hunt
48 Fruit that has a lot of seeds
49 Peg used by a golfer

34

ACROSS

1 Black-eyed ___ (vegetables)
5 "But when ___ got there, the cupboard was bare ..."
8 Soft, sticky stuff
11 "At ___" ("Relax," in the military)
12 Sea creature that's long and thin
13 Go faster than walking
14 Female character in the "Star Wars" movies: 2 words
17 ___ and don'ts
18 "You are what you ___"
19 Little devil
22 The Civil ___
24 Stoops down
28 Fly high
30 "That's really something!"
32 Knocked for a ___ (really surprised)
33 The best possible grade: 2 words
35 The sound a woodpecker makes on a tree
37 24-hour period
38 Slowly ___ surely
40 Settle into a chair
42 Blob-like character in the "Star Wars" movies: 3 words

48 Bird in "Winnie-the-Pooh"
49 Say something that isn't true
50 Japan's continent
51 Honey maker
52 ___ the way (had everyone else follow behind)
53 "What do you ___ from me?"

DOWN

1 Word before "talk" or "squad"
2 Part of the body with a lobe
3 "___ always say ...": 2 words
4 Button on a fax machine
5 Teeter-totter
6 "___ Got the Whole World in His Hands" (song)
7 Something ___ (not this)
8 Hansel's sister
9 How to say "yes" in French
10 Go ___ wild-goose chase: 2 words
15 What Jack traded for magic beans, in "Jack and the Beanstalk"

16 Room where people study chemistry

19 "This ___ surprise!": 2 words

20 You can clean the floor with it

21 Chum

23 Decay

25 Show that you agree

26 ___ good deed (be helpful): 2 words

27 I ___ (game of observation)

29 Barney and Betty's last name, on "The Flintstones"

31 Had a bath

34 Ship that can shoot torpedoes

36 Boston cream ___

39 Not short

41 Melt

42 "This is a ___ for Superman!"

43 Sense of wonder and amazement

44 Score of 3 to 3, for example

45 Country south of Canada: Abbreviation

46 ___ can (kind of container)

47 "I tawt I taw a puddy ___!"

35

ACROSS

1 ___ Blanc (man who was the voice of Porky Pig)
4 Beef or pork, for example
8 What Rembrandt made
11 Tool for a lumberjack
12 What you scratch
13 "___ a minute!"
15 Channel that shows "The Real World": Abbreviation
16 Piano-playing boy in "Peanuts"
18 "You ___ the boss of me!"
20 "___ the fields we go" (line in "Jingle Bells")
21 "I ___ bear of very little brain" (quote from Winnie-the-Pooh): 2 words
22 When prices are marked down
23 Money that has to be paid back
24 Person who's not a Democrat: Abbreviation
25 "That's ___ bad" ("What a shame")
27 Doll or ball, for example
29 Where science experiments take place

32 Cards with just one spot in the center
34 Is in a play
38 Everything
39 "Br'er Rabbit and the ___ Baby"
40 Big city in Nebraska
41 Bird in "Peanuts"
44 Pull, like a broken-down car
45 "Go away!"
46 ___ Krabappel (Bart Simpson's teacher)
47 Ending for "Vietnam"
48 They are used to sell things
49 Say something isn't true
50 Cherry's color

DOWN

1 Mothers
2 ___ large (T-shirt size)
3 On the ___ (truthful)
4 Light fog
5 Abbreviation that could make a list shorter
6 Sneeze sound
7 They might end with the words "or else!"
8 In ___ of (amazed by)

9 Device that can monitor where airplanes are

10 "___ Kangaroo Down, Sport" (song): 2 words

14 You can catch an animal in one

17 Yes ___ (answer choices): 2 words

19 Fish catcher, sometimes

23 Found

26 Grain that's fed to horses

28 Vegetable similar to a sweet potato

29 Illegal things break them

30 "Hello," in Honolulu

31 What the heart pumps

33 Slowly wear away, like the coastline

35 Provide food for a party

36 "Just one of ___ things"

37 Cut a piece of wood

40 "That's fine"

42 Two, in Spanish

43 Cable channel that focuses on news: Abbreviation

36

ACROSS

1 You could take a bath in one
4 "Fun for all ___" (words on some game boxes)
8 Pecans, for example
12 Ending for "Siam"
13 It holds a pet bird
14 "What's ___ for me?": 2 words
15 Container that someone might bring into the school cafeteria
17 ___ beans
18 Big serving spoon
19 "Pumpkin eater" from the nursery rhyme
20 As well
21 Grizzly ___
24 Word ending that means "most"
25 Container that someone might bring into the school cafeteria
28 Weep
31 "___, meeny, miney, mo"
32 White-faced
36 Nut from an oak tree
38 Cut into tiny squares
39 Ripped apart

40 Container that someone might bring into the school cafeteria: 2 words
43 Last word of a hymn
44 Big animals that look like yaks
45 Wife of Adam
46 Home in a tree
47 Result of a small car accident
48 Opposite of no

DOWN

1 "I cannot ___ lie": 2 words
2 Normal
3 Leans over
4 Dull pain
5 Chatter
6 A modest person has a small one
7 Gender
8 The world's longest river
9 Bring together
10 "The New York ___" (famous newspaper)
11 Beginning
16 What the blood will eventually do when you cut yourself

19 ___ and con (the "yes" and "no" sides in a debate)

21 It lives in a hive

22 Ending for "east" or "west"

23 Girl in Louisa May Alcott's "Little Women"

26 Animal that lays eggs

27 Sharp thing that a cowboy wears on a boot

28 The Devil

29 "___ All Ye Faithful" (Christmas carol): 2 words

30 People who aren't very interesting

33 Westminster ___ (London landmark)

34 "I can take it or ___ it"

35 Swords have sharp ones

37 People who live in apartments pay it

38 Penny

40 Pea container

41 Tool used by the Tin Woodman in "The Wizard of Oz"

42 It contains ink

ACROSS

1 ___ Turner (famous singer)
5 Not good
8 Small argument
12 "Don't have ___, man!" (Bart Simpson line): 2 words
13 Country next to Mexico: Abbreviation
14 Group of three singers
15 Brand of soft, spongy ball
16 ___ station (where to put fuel in a car)
17 "Today ___ man" (what a Jewish boy says during his bar mitzvah): 3 words
18 Sit-___ (exercises for the stomach muscles)
20 A unicorn has one
22 Pay-TV
25 ___ rally (school spirit event)
26 They play music: Abbreviation
29 Every last one
30 Really love
32 Dine
33 Hawaiian ring of flowers worn around the neck
34 Feline
35 Like a dweeb
37 High school student, for example
39 "Do ___ say!": 2 words
40 Kind of puzzle
42 Prisoner
44 "How does that ___ you?" ("How do you like that?")
48 Cain and ___ (brothers in the Bible)
49 Opposite of "start"
50 "Dr. Jekyll and Mr. ___"
51 People write with them
52 ___ of sunlight
53 It might be true-false or multiple-choice

DOWN

1 You can get one at the beach
2 It makes a beverage cold
3 Neither this ___ that
4 Really, really bad
5 Creatures with six legs
6 Busy ___ beaver: 2 words
7 One of Santa's reindeer

8 Mix

9 One of Santa's reindeer

10 Point a gun

11 Come ___ conclusion (finish): 2 words

19 What the dove is a symbol of

21 Unlocks

22 Los Angeles's state: Abbreviation

23 Ginger ___

24 One of Santa's reindeer

25 You can boil water in it

27 Father

28 Hog's home

31 One of Santa's reindeer

36 Half of sixteen

38 Slippery swimmers

39 Raggedy ___ (boy doll)

40 It shows you how to get from one place to another

41 Husband of First Lady Mary Todd Lincoln

43 Go ___ vacation: 2 words

45 Dark-colored bread

46 Commercials

47 "You ___ your boots!" ("Absolutely!")

38

ACROSS

1 "___ silly question, get a silly answer": 2 words
5 First, second, or third, on a baseball diamond
9 What a dunce might be forced to wear
12 Building that's used to store tools
13 Put ___ writing: 2 words
14 Encouraging word at a bullfight
15 Gymnast's stunt
17 Container for coal
18 Wipe the chalk off the blackboard
19 Noisy thing on top of an ambulance
21 Member of Congress: Abbreviation
22 ___ rain (environmental problem)
26 "Too ___ cooks spoil the broth"
27 Tampa's state
29 Created
32 Root ___ (kind of drink)
33 Fuel for a car
36 Zodiac sign that follows Pisces
38 Car company that makes the Integra
40 Piece of wood in a woodpile
41 Gymnast's stunt

45 Large, flightless bird
46 Continent next to Europe
47 "Money ___ everything!"
48 Sticky stuff that's used to make syrup
49 What someone in a wheelchair uses instead of stairs
50 Elementary school groups: Abbreviation

DOWN

1 Stuff that's left over at the bottom of a barbecue
2 What a selfish person doesn't want to do
3 "___ & Kel" (Nickelodeon comedy show)
4 Does sums
5 Not the least ___ (not at all)
6 "Now playing ___ theater near you!": 2 words
7 Something that a religion tells you is bad to do
8 Go to the ___ of the Earth
9 Snake that has a "hood"
10 Martian, for example

11 Coin with Lincoln's portrait on the front

16 Animal with flippers and whiskers

20 "___ little teapot, short and stout ...": 2 words

23 Corn's place

24 Country near England: Abbreviation

25 "Cross my heart and hope to ___"

27 What something costs

28 Make a picture

29 Men

30 Smell

31 Find with a shovel: 2 words

33 "Be my ___!" ("Feel free!")

34 Sports coliseum

35 Puts a white seasoning on top of

37 The villain in "The Lion King"

39 "He's a ___ off the old block"

42 Clean ___ whistle: 2 words

43 The edge of a drinking glass

44 Kind of dancing where people have noisemakers on their shoes

39

ACROSS

1 ___ and forth
5 Beef ___ (hearty meal)
9 Something that hurts
10 The North ___ (where Santa lives)
11 Fast plane
14 What you carry food on, in a cafeteria
15 Opposite of hate
16 Bride and groom's words: 2 words
17 ___ Majesty (how people refer to a queen)
18 Destiny
19 They might be scrambled or hard-boiled
20 Not stupid
22 Actors perform on them
24 Valuable card in many games
25 Ocean that borders Florida: Abbreviation
26 Cold season
29 Actors perform in them
31 Comes up with a total
32 Like Darth Vader
34 Desktop machines, for short
36 First name that could be for either a boy or a girl
37 Think ahead
38 Fight with swords
39 Material used in road-paving
40 ___ and rave (shout wildly)
41 The point ___ return: 2 words
42 You see with them
43 Just ___ (not many): 2 words

DOWN

1 Take a ___ (get clean)
2 Farmers measure their land in these units
3 Pokémon character
4 Door opener
5 Sound of a water balloon
6 Horn's sound
7 Santa's helpers
8 ___ Willie Winkie
11 Pokémon character

1	2	3	4		5	6	7	8				
9					10					11	12	13
14					15					16		
17				18					19			
	20		21				22	23				
		24						25				
26	27			28		29					30	
31				32	33				34			35
36			37					38				
39			40					41				
			42					43				

12 Cutting part of a knife
13 Throw
18 ___ throw (one-point shot in basketball)
19 "I'm so hungry I could ___ horse!": 2 words
21 ___ up (misbehaves)
23 Like a giant
26 Mr. Disney
27 "I've got a bright ___"
28 ___ race

29 Parts of a quart
30 Make a ___ (throw a tantrum in public)
33 Weather ___ (thing on top of some roofs)
35 "___ and steady wins the race"
37 Prefix that means "before"
38 ___ good turn (be a good Samaritan): 2 words

40

ACROSS

1 Wild West show
6 "How ___ look?" ("Are my clothes okay?"): 2 words
9 "___ crying out loud!"
12 Ring ___ (sound familiar): 2 words
13 Tall, dark, ___ handsome
14 She's covered in wool
15 City in southern Florida
16 Saturday and Sunday
18 White bird
20 ___ Jose, California
21 "A fool and his money ___ soon parted"
23 Have an ___ for music (be musically talented)
25 Carbonated drinks
29 James ___ (famous movie spy)
31 "I'm on ___ of the world!"
33 "Those ___ the days"
34 They are used in secret messages
36 Candy ___
38 "And many more": Abbreviation
39 ___-Cone (frosty treat)
41 Person who's very weak
43 It holds up volumes on a shelf

47 What people see out of windows
50 Bird that eats mice
51 Card without a number or a face on it
52 Little Orphan ___
53 Get up on the wrong side of the ___
54 Friend of Barbie
55 Shelf

DOWN

1 ___ into (hit head-on)
2 ___-Wan Kenobi ("Star Wars" character)
3 Street that doesn't go anywhere: 2 words
4 Ticklish "Sesame Street" character
5 ___ Oyl (woman in "Popeye")
6 "See-saw, Margery ___" (nursery rhyme)
7 The number 11 contains two of them
8 "Got any more bright ___?"
9 What a lawyer charges
10 Get a taste of your ___ medicine

11 Apple's color, often

17 "Well, what do you ___!"

19 "___ my shorts!" (line from Bart Simpson)

21 Letters before D

22 Kanga's child, in "Winnie-the-Pooh"

24 Be a criminal

26 Part of a swimming pool that isn't shallow: 2 words

27 What a painter creates

28 Part of a minute: Abbreviation

30 Where you sit in a classroom

32 Dog's foot

35 Walk around secretly

37 Opponent in a sport

40 Just a single time

42 Where people dig for coal

43 ___ for apples (play a Halloween game)

44 Have debts

45 ___ as the hills

46 Home for a lion

48 Fake hair

49 Look at

ANSWERS

1

D	A	M		L	A	S	T		S	L	A	P
A	L	I		A	S	K	A		P	E	S	O
R	O	N		T	H	I	N	M	I	N	T	S
T	H	E	S	E			A	N	D	R	E	
H	A	S	A		I	S	A	Y		S	O	S
			D	O	S	I	D	O	S			
A	B	C		V	A	N	S		A	C	T	S
L	L	A	M	A			E	T	H	E	L	
T	A	G	A	L	O	N	G	S		A	X	E
A	M	E	N		W	E	E	P		S	A	P
R	E	D	S		E	V	E	N		E	S	T

2

P	A	N		T	A	P			S	A	Y	
A	G	E	S		I	T	O		N	I	N	E
D	O	D	O		L	A	P		A	D	D	S
	F	L	A	T		E	D	G	E			
C	O	L	O	N		B	Y	A		S	E	A
O	N	A		G	R	E	E	N		H	A	T
B	E	N		L	I	D		C	H	O	R	E
			D	Y	E	S		M	E	O	W	
I	D	E	A		I	D	O		O	B	E	Y
F	O	R	K		N	O	S		D	O	V	E
I	T	S			G	E	T			B	E	T

3

T	A	P	E	S		W	I	T		J	U	G
O	P	E	R	A		O	N	A		U	S	A
M	E	R	I	T		M	A	X		P	E	P
			C	U	R	E		I	F	I		
J	A	M		R	U	N	S		A	T	I	T
O	C	E	A	N	S		T	U	X	E	D	O
N	E	R	D		T	E	A	R		R	O	W
			C	D	S		G	R	A	B		
I	O	U		M	A	Y		N	E	I	G	H
T	A	R		E	S	P		U	N	T	I	E
S	K	Y		E	A	T		S	T	O	N	E

4

M	E	A		H	A	L	F		T	A	G	S
R	E	N		A	S	I	A		O	R	E	O
S	K	I		H	A	L	L	O	W	E	E	N
	M	E	A	N		C	N	N				
T	R	A	Y			D	O	C		A	N	D
V	A	L	E	N	T	I	N	E	S	D	A	Y
S	T	S		E	W	E			E	D	G	E
			A	S	I		L	I	A	R		
C	H	R	I	S	T	M	A	S		E	N	D
B	O	A	R		C	A	N	E		S	I	R
S	E	W	S		H	Y	D	E		S	P	Y

5

B	I	B		R	O	B	E		T	R	A	Y
A	G	E		I	N	O	N		H	O	P	E
H	O	T	C	O	C	O	A		E	W	E	S
			R	T	E		M	E	N			
R	U	L	E			E	E	L		A	S	I
S	N	O	W	B	A	L	L	F	I	G	H	T
T	O	W		A	R	M		B	O	Y	S	
			E	T	C		A	T	E			
S	W	A	N		T	O	B	O	G	G	A	N
H	A	R	D		I	N	A	N		A	L	E
E	Y	E	S		C	O	D	E		B	I	T

6

C	O	U	L	D		A	D	D		K	I	T
A	N	N	I	E		C	I	A		E	M	U
R	O	O	S	E	V	E	L	T		N	A	G
			A	D	E		L	E	A	N		
M	E	L		S	I	P		S	P	E	A	K
E	V	I	L		L	A	D		E	D	G	E
G	E	N	E	S		Y	E	S		Y	E	N
			C	O	A	T		A	T	E		
D	O	O		J	E	F	F	E	R	S	O	N
O	W	L		A	L	L		P	I	A	N	O
T	E	N		K	E	Y		S	E	W	E	R

7

```
DADS BOP  STAY
IBET RIO  ERIE
MUSICALCHAIRS
  CUT  KIT
AWAKE PET  RAP
CAPS MAT  CASE
EYE  OAT  WOMAN
  ELM  IAM
BLINDMANSBUFF
BEND ART  ASIA
SEAS LEO  TENT
```

8

```
MOSS TOCK WOW
EWOK ECHO EWE
ALLIGATOR ANT
  PAR  PETS
HAT BUT  AHEAD
ATOP PER  ELMO
SMURF NEW  SIT
  COAT AHA
ASH CROCODILE
TOE TENT  DOES
END SEES  SUIT
```

9

```
APIE ARMS PRO
DADA PARK REP
DIETPEPSI IVE
 NASA  MANIN
  WASH  ICES
 MOUNTAINDEW
TOMS ANDA
OBESE  MUSH
TIL SCHWEPPES
OLE PURE  TART
PET NEST  ONES
```

10

```
BATHE EBB
ACORN ALL  SON
GHOST SUE  ABE
SET EATEN  NOR
 HORSE  DATED
SOFA ARM  MASS
APART BASIC
FRI UTURN  LUG
EAR SAN  ACARE
SHY KIN  ROUGE
  SLY  LOSES
```

11

```
BOAST FEE  SIP
INDIA RAT  ACE
TEETH ETC  NEW
  SIGN  HOT
DOI TAC  FAST
ENGLISHMUFFIN
SANE TAN  ENT
 ODD  ONTO
JAR ASA  IVORY
AGE YES  EARED
NOD SET  SLEDS
```

12

```
  FAST  ACES
CAP ARCH  MILK
UNO WEAR  ANTI
PECAN REP  DOE
SWAY FEAR  END
 HERO  DOOR
MOO ARMS  WERE
UPN GEE  ALLEY
SETA STAG  LEE
IRAN TAPE  ADS
CAST SLED
```

13

R	U	B		G	O	T		R	A	D	A	R
A	S	A		R	I	O		O	P	E	R	A
G	E	R	M	A	N	Y		P	I	N	K	Y
		A	S	K		S	E	E	M			
B	A	I	T	S		B	U	S		A	G	E
O	G	R	E		R	U	N		W	R	E	N
P	O	E		P	I	G		P	O	K	E	D
	L	A	I	D		S	A	N				
S	T	A	R	E		A	U	S	T	R	I	A
O	W	N	E	R		H	I	T		A	C	T
S	O	D	A	S		A	T	A		W	E	E

14

B	I	D		L	A	S	T		J	A	M
U	N	O		A	B	E	E		S	U	R	E
S	K	I	T	T	L	E	S		I	J	K	L
	W	E	E		T	U	T	U			
L	E	G	O		P	E	P		B	I	G
A	G	O		M	A	I	D	S		E	M	U
B	O	O		A	N	T		E	S	P	N
	B	O	Y	S		G	A	S			
B	L	E	W		W	H	O	P	P	E	R	S
E	A	R	N		E	U	R	O		Y	O	U
A	D	S		R	E	E	D		E	W	E

15

F	A	S	T		I	F	I		F	A	T
I	R	O	N		T	H	I	N		I	D	O
L	I	N	T		E	A	R	N		R	O	O
L	E	I		E	N	D	S		J	E	R	K
	S	C	O	L	D		T	R	A	D	E
		U	S	E		C	O	W			
	W	A	T	E	R		L	O	S	E	R
W	E	D	S		F	L	A	T		V	A	T
H	A	D		T	O	E	S		M	E	N	U
E	V	E		R	O	S	S		U	R	G	E
N	E	D		I	T	S		D	Y	E	S

16

P	A	W	S		T	R	A	P		B	A	G
U	T	A	H		H	E	R	O		U	P	A
T	O	T	O		E	X	T	R	E	M	E	S
	E	T	C			T	A	P			
P	A	R		A	B	A	T		R	E	A	L
E	S	S		T	E	X	A	S		R	B	I
G	I	L	A		N	E	C	K		B	E	D
	I	T	S		I	D	O				
S	I	D	E	W	A	L	K		E	A	S	T
A	C	E		A	L	I	E		S	T	A	R
Y	E	S		P	I	T	Y		I	S	P	Y

17

P	I	G		E	G	G		P	A	S	T
A	R	E		L	O	A	F		E	L	E	E
P	I	T		M	O	P	E		S	O	L	E
A	S	T	R	O	S		A	U	T	U	M	N
S	H	O	O		E	A	R	N		D	A	Y
		B	A	B	Y	S	I	T			
S	I	S		D	U	E	T		A	S	A	N
A	N	T	H	E	M		R	I	P	P	L	E
I	D	E	A		P	O	E	T		R	O	W
L	I	A	R		S	U	E	S		A	N	T
S	A	M	E		S	T	Y		Y	E	S

18

H	O	T		B	E	L	L		A	D	A	Y
O	U	R		A	R	E	A		B	O	N	E
P	T	A		K	I	T	T	Y	C	A	T	S
	F	R	E	E		H	E	S			
S	A	F	E	R		W	E	T		C	O	P
A	C	I	D		C	A	R		T	U	N	A
D	E	C		B	R	R		M	O	R	A	L
	S	U	E		A	I	M	S			
P	U	P	P	Y	D	O	G	S		I	S	A
A	S	I	A		I	B	E	T		V	A	N
W	A	N	T		T	I	D	Y		E	N	D

19

```
BAGS  OVER  ■ ■
ALOT  FIVE  TRA
LILY  FEED  HOT
LED  DAWN  PROM
■ NICE  STREET
■ LOST  SORE ■
■ LOOKED  CUBA
TICK  RISK  ERN
OAK  IRAN  SALE
MRS  NONO  CREW
■ CRAB  ISNT
```

20

```
ALSO  ADS  ACTS
TOTE  BET  HERE
OVER  ONE  AMEN
PEA  OUTER  EAT
■ SMART  PAINT
■ RID  TNT
■ CORES  TEAMS
PAL  RACES  ITS
LILY  COD  EXIT
AREA  KID  GENE
YORK  SLY  GREW
```

21

```
■ SEAM  IGOT
ASH  HERO  TORE
DOI  EYES  ABEE
ARTS  OATS  ESS
METEORS  OLD
■ SHAPE  MAIDS
■ ESE  CARRYON
LAS  NOON  ABLE
ISAW  ARAB  YES
DICE  RAGU  EST
SAKE  SLED ■
```

22

```
LAG  CAP  HAUL
ESE  IDO  ALSO
GHOSTSTORIES
■ RAY  TOM
BAGGY  PEP  BAA
APIE  NOR  EARN
TEN  ROD  HIRED
■ AIR  MUG
PILLOWFIGHTS
OVAL  AAS  TEA
PEWS  YRS  YET
```

23

```
LOW  FORTS  FEW
INA  ALERT  IVE
PET  MEDIA  NED
■ EWE  DRAG
CURE  BEE  MEAN
ONCE  RAN  URGE
TOON  ART  SPOT
■ LYNX  PEA
UFO  ATARI  ITS
PER  GOTIN  NOT
ADS  SNAPS  TOY
```

24

```
LAPS  MUGS  FOG
EXIT  AFRO  LIE
XENA  GOOFBALL
■ BRAG  WAY
ASA  RIB  EELS
GAL  FEAST  YOU
OWLS  ATA  EWE
■ AOL  ARAB
MEATBALL  PAUL
IVY  EVIL  ELSE
SEE  YAPS  SLED
```

25

C	H	A	T		S	H	E		M	A	T	E
A	B	L	E		O	I	L		A	L	E	G
R	O	L	L	E	R	S	K	A	T	I	N	G
		L	A	T		S	I	T				
T	V	S		T	O	P		M	E	D	A	L
A	C	E	S		F	A	T		L	O	B	E
G	R	E	A	T		W	E	D		G	E	T
			Y	E	S		T	O	A			
M	I	N	I	A	T	U	R	E	G	O	L	F
A	T	O	N		A	S	I		E	R	I	E
R	A	N	G		G	A	S		S	E	E	D

26

R	H	I	N	O		F	R	O		S	H	E
A	B	O	U	T		L	I	T		H	E	Y
M	O	U	N	T	R	U	S	H	M	O	R	E
			S	E	A		K	E	E	P		
B	I	G		R	I	D		R	A	P	I	D
U	T	A	H		L	O	G		L	E	N	O
D	A	R	E	D		G	A	S		R	A	T
			D	R	E	W		N	O	W		
T	H	E	E	V	E	R	G	L	A	D	E	S
R	A	N		I	V	E		O	L	I	V	E
I	T	S		L	E	D		S	L	E	E	T

27

F	A	T		P	A	S	S		I	R	A	N
A	B	E		R	I	O	T		L	U	R	E
C	E	N	T	E	R	F	I	E	L	D	E	R
E	L	S	E		S	A	N	D		E	N	D
S	L	E	E	P		S	K	I		R	A	Y
			S	U	B		S	T	Y			
N	O	D		T	O	T		S	A	L	E	M
A	P	E		O	R	A	L		L	I	M	A
S	E	C	O	N	D	B	A	S	E	M	A	N
T	R	A	Y		E	L	M	O		B	I	D
Y	A	L	L		R	E	E	L		S	L	Y

28

L	A	C	E		A	P	E	S				
I	N	O	N		C	A	V	E		R	A	T
N	E	R	D		T	R	E	E		A	L	E
D	E	N		O	R	E		S	M	I	L	E
A	L	F		W	E	D	S		A	S	I	N
			L	E	N	S		T	A	X	I	
P	R	A	Y		S	P	U	N		N	A	B
L	A	K	E	S		A	D	D		B	R	R
A	C	E		L	I	V	E		A	R	E	A
Y	E	S		O	V	E	N		H	A	N	G
			B	E	S	T		A	N	T	S	

29

A	H	A		R	O	B		S	P	R	A	T
L	O	W		I	V	E		K	O	A	L	A
A	P	E		F	A	N	T	A	S	T	I	C
		S	E	L	L		A	T	E			
C	R	O	W	E		P	I	E		A	S	A
D	O	M	E		D	E	L		S	M	O	G
E	Y	E		W	E	T		P	E	A	S	E
			O	R	A		D	I	A	Z		
W	O	N	D	E	R	F	U	L		I	T	A
O	N	E	I	N		A	D	E		N	O	R
W	A	D	E	S		R	E	D		G	O	T

30

	A	C	R	E		N	O	T		A	B	C
A	C	H	E	S		I	N	A		P	E	A
T	H	E	S	P	I	C	E	G	I	R	L	S
M	O	S	T		D	E	S		C	O	L	T
S	O	S		P	E	R		P	A	N	E	S
			B	A	A		J	A	N			
S	A	N	E	R		M	A	D		C	P	R
O	R	A	L		S	A	W		S	H	O	O
D	E	S	T	I	N	Y	S	C	H	I	L	D
A	N	T		C	O	B		B	O	N	E	S
S	A	Y		E	W	E		S	E	A	S	

31

G	I	J	O	E		A	B	S		D	I	L
U	T	U	R	N		G	O	O		O	N	E
T	A	M	E	D		O	W	N		U	N	O
		P	O	E	M		L	I	M	B		
A	M	I		D	A	M		C	O	L	O	R
S	E	N	T		D	O	C		W	E	R	E
A	N	G	E	L		P	A	C		D	E	N
		R	A	I	N		R	A	G	U		
P	R	O		M	O	B		I	N	T	H	E
R	A	P		O	N	A		R	A	C	E	R
E	Y	E		S	E	T		O	T	H	E	R

32

L	A	B		U	S	E	R		A	M	A	N
A	S	A		P	A	V	E		G	O	R	E
W	E	B		S	H	E	S		O	W	E	S
S	A	Y	S		A	N	T	S		I	N	S
	T	S	H	I	R	T		P	A	N	T	
	I	O	W	A		S	A	N	G			
	I	T	T	O		C	A	M	E	L	S	
T	N	T		N	E	R	D		W	A	T	T
I	D	I	D		D	U	D	S		W	A	Y
P	I	N	E		I	D	E	A		N	I	P
S	A	G	S		T	E	R	M		S	N	O

33

A	S	K	S		O	L	D		K	A	T	E
T	H	E	O		N	O	R		A	L	O	T
M	E	T	S		I	S	A		Z	I	N	C
		C	O	L	O		T	W	O			
A	S	H		I	N	A		H	O	M	E	S
A	P	U		A	S	T	R	O		U	G	H
H	Y	P	E	R		E	E	L		S	O	Y
		T	S	P		L	E	F	T			
W	I	T	H		A	M	I		R	A	F	T
O	D	I	E		L	A	S		E	R	I	E
N	O	E	L		M	P	H		E	D	G	E

34

P	E	A	S		S	H	E		G	O	O	
E	A	S	E		E	E	L		R	U	N	
P	R	I	N	C	E	S	S	L	E	I	A	
			D	O	S		E	A	T			
I	M	P		W	A	R		B	E	N	D	S
S	O	A	R		W	O	W		L	O	O	P
A	P	L	U	S		T	A	P		D	A	Y
		B	U	T		S	I	T				
J	A	B	B	A	T	H	E	H	U	T	T	
O	W	L		L	I	E		A	S	I	A	
B	E	E		L	E	D		W	A	N	T	

35

M	E	L		M	E	A	T		A	R	T	
A	X	E		I	T	C	H		W	A	I	T
M	T	V		S	C	H	R	O	E	D	E	R
A	R	E	N	T		O	E	R		A	M	A
S	A	L	E		L	O	A	N		R	E	P
		T	O	O		T	O	Y				
L	A	B		A	C	E	S		A	C	T	S
A	L	L		T	A	R		O	M	A	H	A
W	O	O	D	S	T	O	C	K		T	O	W
S	H	O	O		E	D	N	A		E	S	E
	A	D	S		D	E	N	Y		R	E	D

36

T	U	B		A	G	E	S		N	U	T	S
E	S	E		C	A	G	E		I	N	I	T
L	U	N	C	H	B	O	X		L	I	M	A
L	A	D	L	E			P	E	T	E	R	
A	L	S	O		B	E	A	R		E	S	T
			T	H	E	R	M	O	S			
S	O	B		E	E	N	Y		P	A	L	E
A	C	O	R	N		C	U	B	E	D		
T	O	R	E		P	A	P	E	R	B	A	G
A	M	E	N		O	X	E	N		E	V	E
N	E	S	T		D	E	N	T		Y	E	S

37

T	I	N	A		B	A	D		S	P	A	T
A	C	O	W		U	S	A		T	R	I	O
N	E	R	F		G	A	S		I	A	M	A
			U	P	S		H	O	R	N		
C	A	B	L	E		P	E	P		C	D	S
A	L	L		A	D	O	R	E		E	A	T
L	E	I		C	A	T		N	E	R	D	Y
	T	E	E	N		A	S	I				
M	A	Z	E		C	O	N		G	R	A	B
A	B	E	L		E	N	D		H	Y	D	E
P	E	N	S		R	A	Y		T	E	S	T

38

A	S	K	A		B	A	S	E		C	A	P
S	H	E	D		I	T	I	N		O	L	E
H	A	N	D	S	T	A	N	D		B	I	N
E	R	A	S	E			S	I	R	E	N	
S	E	N		A	C	I	D		M	A	N	Y
		F	L	O	R	I	D	A				
M	A	D	E		B	E	E	R		G	A	S
A	R	I	E	S			A	C	U	R	A	
L	O	G		C	A	R	T	W	H	E	E	L
E	M	U		A	S	I	A		I	S	N	T
S	A	P		R	A	M	P		P	T	A	S

39

B	A	C	K		S	T	E	W				
A	C	H	E		P	O	L	E		J	E	T
T	R	A	Y		L	O	V	E		I	D	O
H	E	R		F	A	T	E		E	G	G	S
	S	M	A	R	T		S	T	A	G	E	S
	A	C	E			A	T	L				
W	I	N	T	E	R		P	L	A	Y	S	
A	D	D	S		E	V	I	L		P	C	S
L	E	E		P	L	A	N		D	U	E	L
T	A	R		R	A	N	T		O	F	N	O
			E	Y	E	S		A	F	E	W	

40

R	O	D	E	O		D	O	I		F	O	R
A	B	E	L	L		A	N	D		E	W	E
M	I	A	M	I		W	E	E	K	E	N	D
	D	O	V	E		S	A	N				
A	R	E		E	A	R		S	O	D	A	S
B	O	N	D		T	O	P		W	E	R	E
C	O	D	E	S		B	A	R		E	T	C
	S	N	O		W	I	M	P				
B	O	O	K	E	N	D		V	I	E	W	S
O	W	L		A	C	E		A	N	N	I	E
B	E	D		K	E	N		L	E	D	G	E

ABOUT THE AUTHOR

When he was a kid, Trip Payne was addicted to crossword puzzles—so much so that he tried making them on his own. He had a few published in school newspapers, then finally had one published in *Games Magazine* when he was 15 years old, and he's been in the puzzle business ever since. Aside from the *Crosswords for Kids* series, he has made kids' puzzles for such publications as *Scholastic News*, *Games Junior*, and *Zigzag*.

Dan Wenke at Bern-Art Studios

WHAT IS AMERICAN MENSA?

American Mensa
The High IQ Society
One out of 50 people qualifies
for American Mensa ...
Are YOU the One?

American Mensa, Ltd. is an organization for individuals who have one common trait: a score in the top two percent of the population on a standardized intelligence test. Over five million Americans are eligible for membership ... you may be one of them.

• Looking for intellectual stimulation?
You'll find a good "mental workout" in the *Mensa Bulletin*, our national magazine. Voice your opinion in the newsletter published by your local group. And attend activities and gatherings with fascinating programs and engaging conversation.

• Looking for social interaction?
There's something happening on the Mensa calendar almost daily. These range from lectures to game nights to parties. Each year, there are over 40 regional gatherings and the Annual Gathering, where you can meet people, exchange ideas, and make interesting new friends.

• Looking for others who share your special interest?

Whether your interest might be computer gaming, the meaning of life, science fiction & fantasy, or scuba diving, there's probably a Mensa Special Interest Group (SIG) for you. There are over 150 SIGs, maintained by members just in the United States.

So visit our Web site for more information about American Mensa Ltd.

http://www.us.mensa.org

Or call our automated messaging system to request an application or for additional information:

(800) 66-MENSA

Or write to us at:

American Mensa Ltd.
1229 Corporate Drive West
Arlington, TX 76006
AmericanMensa@mensa.org

If you don't live in the United States and would like to get in touch with your national Mensa organization, contact:

Mensa International
15 The Ivories
6–8 Northampton Street, Islington
London N1 2HY England
www.mensa.org